How To Sell Your Home By Owner

How To Sell Your Home By Owner

(Investor Secrets)

Dave Perkins

Library of Congress Control Number:		2010917012
ISBN:	Hardcover	978-1-4568-1559-2
	Softcover	978-1-4568-1464-9
	Ebook	978-1-4568-1465-6

This book was printed in the United States of America.

To order additional copies of this book, contact:
Xlibris Corporation
1-888-795-4274
www.Xlibris.com
Orders@Xlibris.com
89965

Contents

PREFACE

IN THIS BOOK; you will learn how to sell your home quickly and for top dollar. You will learn how to sell it faster than you may have dreamed possible.

The book covers preparing your home for sale, advertising, finding buyers, showing your home to buyers, qualifying buyers, and finally the people and processes needed to close your home sale.

I will share with you different types of home buyers, and which ones are most likely to buy your home. Once you know this, you can target your advertising accordingly. You will be able to find buyers real estate agents do not find. The people most likely to buy may surprise you.

You will be able to help your buyers find financing and you will learn financing techniques that will have potential buyers lining up at your door.

Please bookmark the website below, and use it in conjunction with this book. It contains links for most of the processes you'll need to successfully sell your home.

www.davepinvestments.com

CHAPTER 1

Pricing your Home

I F YOU ALREADY have an appraisal you may want to skip this chapter. However, if it has been more than a few months since your home has been appraised, you might want to revisit the amount once more, as comparables in your area may have changed.

Using these techniques, you can determine the market appraisal for your home without requiring a real estate agent or a professional appraiser. Here is how to determine an accurate sales price:

Take Inventory of your homes condition and upgrades

Take a complete inventory of your home in order to do a full and accurate comparison to like properties. At minimum, ask yourself these questions:

- What condition is my home?
- What year was it built?
- How does my yard look?
- How does my home compare to others in the area?
- What upgrades do I have?
- Does my home have hardwood floors?
- What materials are the countertops?
- Have my kitchen appliances been upgraded?

- How old is the furnace?
- How old is the air conditioner?
- How old is the roof?
- Are any repairs needed before selling?

Ask the same questions you will ask when looking for your next home. The answers to these will let you know if you should price your home below or above the average for your area.

Note: This may be a good time for you to fill out the 'Residential Property Disclosure Statement' at the back of this book. This is usually one of the documents required for closing. Even if it's not a requirement in your State; it is a good thing to share with your buyer.

Find Comparables

The homes used for comparisons are called comparables, or comps. To get an accurate picture of what homes are selling for, you want to find as many comps as possible, sold as recently as possible. The number of comps available will depend on how active the market is; but a dozen similar homes, sold within the past few months, will give you an accurate base to calculate your homes market value.

Consider such things as these when determining comps:

- Number of bedrooms
- Square footage
- Price per square footage
- Number of stories and style of home
- Heating and Cooling methods
- Floor coverings
- Cabinet and Appliance types
- Lot size
- Age of Home
- Age of Roof
- Home Location, both in your immediate area and in general (example: is it on a corner, end of street, gravel or paved road? Is it close to Stores? Schools? Etc . . .).

Following are several methods that can be used for finding comps. Keep in mind, the more research you do, and the more comps you find; the more accurate your sales price will be, and the more prepared you'll be to explain to buyers the reasons your home is priced the way it is.

Research in Local Home Buyer Publications

Pick up some of the home sale brochures or booklets at your local market and look to see what the asking price is for homes similar to yours.

Look at homes in your area

Scout your area as though you were buying a home. Notice whether the Home is for sale by owner or through an agent. Record prices, pick up for sale brochures, look up the homes on the realtors sites, etc . . . This may give you the best insight to asking prices for homes similar to yours.

Research Homes for Sale Online

Today, the best method to find comparable prices is online. Following are several sites that may work well for you. Much of what might be available will depend on where you live. Each has a little different content, but all may help you establish your best price. You can search all these sites for free.

www.google.com

If you live in a populated area, you might be surprised at the amount of information Google has pulled from public records on your home. Begin by putting in your address and see what it brings up. You may find property history, including past selling prices. You'll find the asking prices for homes in your area, what nearby homes have sold for in the past six months, what the median house value is . . . and more. In some cases, this may supply you with all the information necessary to determine the asking price for your home. However, if that's not the case, there are other methods you can use.

www.realtors.com.

I like realtors.com, but you can apply this method using practically any real estate site. Let's say you are selling a 3 bd 2 bath 2,000 sq ft home. Looking in the real estate site, do a search on 3 bd 2 bath homes in your City and State. Write down how many there are, and the bottom and top prices. Let's use an example where the low price is $150,000 and the top price is $300,000. Draw a table similar to the one below, and break ranges into incremental values. I am using $25,000 increments for this example. Now perform searches by price increments, still leaving the 3 bd 2 bath in your search criteria, and write in the number of homes in each range.

Range Low	Range High	# Homes
150,000	175,000	5
175,000	200,000	10
200,000	225,000	30
225,000	250,000	40
250,000	275,000	10
275,000	300,000	3

What range(s) are most the homes in your area selling for? In my example, the majority of homes are in the $200,000 to $250,000 range. I can probably assume the closer the homes are to the $250,000, the more upgrades they have. The lower priced homes will most likely need some work, and the median priced are probably average for your neighborhood. Where does your home fit into these prices? Still need more information? Then let's look at additional home details. Do individual searches on the homes that you feel are within your price range, and look at specific details for each home. Build another table showing the specifics of your home in columns. What's the square footage, how big is your lot, how old is your home, calculate the price per square foot at what you think your asking price will be (simply divide the selling price by the square footage). Put the same information for each home you find in additional rows so you end up with a good comparison of the details at a glance. Play with this sheet until you feel you have captured homes that are very similar to yours. This should give you an excellent feeling for what you can ask. Keep in mind, most homes sell at a 4% and 10% discount from the asking price.

www.zillow.com

Similar to Google; Zillow pulls information for public records. Look at: *www.zillow.com/howto/DataCoverageZestimateAccuracy.htm* to see a table showing how accurate the Zillow estimates, called Zestimates, are where you live. The home data compiled to generate a Zestimate home valuation varies by location. Some counties provide all the data Zillow could hope for, but others are lacking such key things as basic as number of bedrooms and bathrooms, or square footage of the home. The more data they have, the more accurate the Zestimate. And, Zillow has made it easier for their users to help improve accuracy by incorporating edited home facts into their Zestimate calculations. In some areas, they might not be able to produce a Zestimate at all, but even then, they do have some basic information on the homes.

www.trulia.com

The next site I want you to look at is trulia.com. This site has home sales where the price has been reduced, New Listings, Foreclosed Listings, Average

Listing Prices, Median Sales Prices, Number of properties sold recently, and percentage of increase or decrease in the value of homes being sold. Some or all of this information may contribute to the determination of your asking price. This will give you good insight to the overall market conditions for your neighborhood.

County Records

And finally, last but not least, is your County website. This usually contains much of the same information as the above sites, but it is sometimes difficult to find your way around your County site since there isn't any continuity between counties. The layout here can vary greatly from County to County. County records will have the last time the house was sold, and the amount. The records will also have the square footage, and tax amounts.

Using these methods, you should have more information than necessary to determine your sales price. Your accuracy may depend on how willing you are to search and compare.

Professional Appraisal

Even after all this research, you may still be required to seek a professional appraisal depending on what type of loan your buyer is getting. But for now, the price you have established should be fine. I expect you will be very close to the professional appraisal amount as well.

Adjust Sale Price

You've now established a preliminary sale price for your home. This allows you to make some marketing strategies based on the price, or adjust your price based on the market in your area.

Adjust Sale Price Based on Marketing Strategy

Most everyone juggles two things to determine their asking price. What they want to net from the sale, and how fast they want the home to sell.

There are however, some additional questions you should ask yourself as you compare your price to the average prices in your area.

- Have I made upgrades? I should be able to move my price up from the average.
- Does my home need work? I can expect to move my price down from the average.

- What are the demographics of my neighborhood? Is it first time homebuyers, families, retirees? Knowing this may help you with targeting your advertising.
- Is my home and area priced within the FHA or Government Home Loan Program Guidelines? I explain how to find these guidelines later in this book. But consider if you are just outside the guidelines, you may want to move within the guidelines to pick up many more potential buyers.

Adjust Price Based on Potential Buyers

If you want to sell your home fast, and for top dollar, it is important you understand the different types of buyers, how their needs and requirements differ, and how you can market to all of them. Here are the types of buyers you may run across as you market your home:

- Good to Excellent Credit, No Financial Challenges, and will probably be pre-approved. Sounds good, doesn't it. This however, may be the most difficult group to sell your home to.
- Good to Excellent Credit, No Financial Challenges, but buying your home could be contingent on selling theirs.
- Good to Excellent Credit, but have some financial challenges. The challenges might be limited cash available for down and closing, or recent loss of income.
- Poor Credit, but has money for the down payment, has a steady job, and can afford the monthly mortgage on your home.
- Poor Credit, and has financial challenges with the down payment or closing costs, but has a steady job, and qualifying income to meet government loan programs.

Which of these would you think would be the most likely to purchase your home? The groups you may want to focus your marketing will probably surprise you. This is your first secret. The best groups may very well be the last two. Knowing this might impact both your time-to-market and your sales price. For now, I want you to think about a couple things:

- Usually, the good to excellent credit buyers will expect you to come down on your original asking price. You can expect your initial asking price will be reduced somewhere between 4% and 10%. Yet this is the market most sellers expect will buy their home.
- On the other hand, the poor credit or cash challenged buyers will usually be happy to pay the full asking price, especially if you can help them with closing costs or a portion of the down payment. You will learn more on this in the chapter 'Qualifying your Buyer'

CHAPTER 2

Prepare for Open House

ALTHOUGH CURB APPEAL may pull buyers into your home, it is most likely the inside that will determine if you get an offer or not. Did you know buyers usually determine whether they are interested in buying a home within the first 15 seconds of stepping inside? It's critical they see a clean, uncluttered, and well organized home; someplace they can visualize themselves living in.

Clean Your Home:

The most important part of home staging is making sure the home is clean and smells good. You want your home look like a model home as much as possible. Buyers simply do not accept excuses. So let's not hear 'but I have pets' or 'but I'm a smoker', or 'but I have kids'. Give your home a top to bottom cleaning. Dust everything, including ceiling fans, windows and floor trim and moldings. You may even want to hire a professional to do this. The good news for many is that it doesn't have to be kept spotless all the time, but it should be a couple times a week, at your open house times, which I'll cover later.

Store your Clutter:

Move out unneeded dishes, linens, personal items and furniture. Be sure to organize drawers. Don't leave dirty dishes in the sink or dishwasher. Buyers will look in them! Remove all cleaning products and sponges from the kitchen sink and counters. Organize the counters with just a few items. Remove magnets, photos or notes attached to the refrigerator. Remove personal pictures and items from walls and table tops. Have very few knickknacks or artworks displayed. If you need to, rent a storage locker for the extra items. Your house will appear larger and more valuable when this is done.

Organize Cupboards and Closets

Little things mean a lot here. Buyers will look in cupboards and closets, and the condition of these will lead to assumptions about the rest of the house. Go as far as alphabetizing spice jars, neatly stacking dishes in the cupboards, even turning coffee cup handles facing the same direction. Hang all the clothes in the closets with the fronts in the same direction, organize shoes. You may go so far as to use all the same types of clothes hangers. If you have anything on the closet shelves, it should be neat and organized.

Make Simple Repairs

It is well worth the minor cost to fix broken outlets, tiles, light switches, door latches, folding doors, and ceiling fans. If you can't do these repairs yourself, look for a handyman in your area. Buyers view such flaws as signs of bigger problems.

Paint

Inside, cover up any blemishes and repaint rooms that are currently in bold colors. Outside, if the house is peeling, scrape it and repaint. Put a fresh coat of paint on shutters and trim if they are dull. Houses with rooms in light colors sell much faster than those with bold more personal colors. Lighter colors also make rooms look bigger and brighter, as well as allowing the buyer to imagine their furniture with the wall colors.

Yard Landscape

At minimum, mow the lawn, edge around sidewalks, weed the flowerbeds, and pull any dying bushes. Plant flowers in bare spots. If you have a porch, be sure it is clean and organized. This is the introduction of your home to buyers. No one likes to see trash, toys, or stuffed furniture on the front porch. If you have an outside sitting area, please be sure you use outdoor furniture! I cannot stress enough the importance of curb appeal. Most buyers will turn away from a home if it doesn't look good on the outside. It needs to fit in with the rest of the neighborhood for you to get your asking price. This probably seems like common sense, but be sure to do this before taking a picture for your advertising! As you look through the ads, you'll notice not everyone does this.

How this differs with different types of Buyers.

This brings us to the next secret: Credit Challenged Buyers will be thrilled you are able to consider them to buy your home, and will not be as bothered by the little things such as outdated color schemes or minor landscaping issues or flaws in a wall. The more qualified buyers, because they are able to consider many homes, will consider these items more as flaws that need to be corrected.

CHAPTER 3

Home Improvements

Good Improvements

I F YOU ARE thinking you might want to do some additional home improvements prior to selling you home; here is a list of best and worst home improvements for your dollar. The National Association of Realtors conducts an annual survey of its members in 80 cities that is used to estimate the return on investment for 33 home improvement projects. The 2009 report concluded that, on average, for every $1,000 spent on projects, the return is $638. Some home improvements thought to be good are:

Hardware Replacement

Cost: $300
You don't want to replace kitchen cabinets or closet doors. But you can upgrade these by installing new handles, knobs and drawer pulls where needed.

New Appliances

Cost: $500 to $1,000
There is no need to upgrade to the latest stainless steel appliances. But a worn stove or refrigerator could scare buyers away. You may want to upgrade these to a budget friendly replacement.

Steel Entry Door

Cost: Around $1,170
Surprisingly, a heavy entry door is one of the upgrades with an impressive return. The estimates say you'll get a 29% gain on your investment.

Roofing Credit

Cost: $19,700
If your roof leaks, offer the buyers a discount. This will likely cost you less than the difference between what it will cost you to replace the roof before selling and the lesser amount you'll recoup afterward.

Improvements to Avoid

I've talked about things you should do to help with the sale. Let's talk some about the upgrades that are not cost effective. You'll notice these are all significant costing projects. The bottom line is, if you want to do these, do them for yourself and your family. They will not bring you good return on your investment.

Adding Family Room

Cost: $82,800
Bottom line; this will not make you a profit when selling your home.

Adding Master Bedroom Suite

Cost: $103,700
Although adding bedrooms will add value to your home, you're likely to lose about one-third of your investment.

Fiberglass Entry Door

Cost: $3,500
Although buyers do appreciate a new door, the high price of fiberglass doesn't justify the additional cost. Stay with the Steel doors as mentioned above.

Adding Garage

Cost: $58,400
Similar to a Master Bedroom Suite; this is a good selling point for the home, but you can expect to lose about one-third of your investment.

Adding Bathroom

Cost: $39,000

The idea the more bathrooms the better has changed. Bottom line is; the bath bubble has burst.

Power Generators

Cost: $14,300

Although this may give buyers peace of mind, you can only expect to recover 40% of your investment

Adding a Sunroom or Porch

Cost: $73,200

These don't come close to justify the cost. You're likely to recover half of your investment

Remodeling Home Office

Cost: $28,400

People don't put much value on walnut bookshelves and built-in desks. In addition, such features make it hard for a buyer to use the space as an additional bedroom.

CHAPTER 4

Advertising

SOMETIMES THE BEST forms of advertising are also the simplest. Especially when selling your home yourself. But don't simply put a sign in your front yard and expect people to come knocking on your door. You need to think like a professional. Your profession is selling your home.

I'm going to introduce some terms; "Creative Financing", "Home Owner Financing", "Poor Credit Ok", "Low Down Payment", "Owner pays closing costs". You should consider these when creating your ads. Using the above terms will pull in customers that other sellers in your area do not. Don't panic, I'll be explaining how you can offer these techniques in later chapters.

You need to be advertising your home to a dozen or so potential buyers a day. This can be done by using several methods of advertising. Using these will grab your customer's attention and let them know you have something to offer other sellers don't. Give yourself a challenge. Do these for thirty days and see if you're not amazed by the responses you receive. Here's what you should do.

Newspaper

Place an ad in your local newspaper. Here is a sample of a good newspaper ad.

CREATIVE FINANCING
3ba 2bd 2,000 sq. ft. Home
Upgraded Kitchen, hardwood floors
Small Down, $800 Monthly
Call Dave 555.55.5555

Of course you will tailor this ad to your home, but have one of the key phrases such as 'Creative Financing' or 'Owner Financing' on the first line. This is the attention getter! Always show the number of bedrooms, baths, and square footage. Of course replace the 'upgraded kitchen, hardwood floors' in my example with some of the best features of your home. Usually, you will want to target your ad to benefits for a family with children or pets. For example: Fenced Yard, Close to Schools, Good Location. Of course this depends on your area. Your area might be best for first time home buyers, or empty nesters, or retirees. When listing your name and phone number; simply list your first name. This seems much more personal and friendlier than a real estate or sales company.

Run your ad for a week or ten days, but always include Sunday. This is the day most buyers look at ads, and scout for homes. If the ad doesn't give you the response you want, change it after the initial running; don't just extend the same ad.

For Sale Signs

Place your primary For Sale Sign with your phone number in front of your home. If your area allows, also place a couple of these signs at street corners near your home. Here's an example of the yard sign verbiage:

FOR SALE BY OWNER
CREATIVE FINANCING
3ba 2bd 2,000 sq. ft. home
Upgraded Kitchen
555-55-5555

If possible, have 3 additional signs at every turn from the main traffic area to the street your home is on. Tell a story as people pass each sign.

Street Sign 1:
"CREATIVE FINANCING"
555-55-5555

Street Sign 2:
"580 CREDIT SCORE, OK"
555-55-555

Street Sign 3:

OPEN HOUSE
Tue: 5:00 – 7:00pm"
Home Address
555-55-555

Use your imagination for these. What attracts buyers to homes in your area? Here are some tips: The signs should be readable from several car lengths away. Hand written signs will work as well, if not better, than pre-printed signs. They should all be the same color and same design so when buyers see the main yard sign, they know this is the correct house. You don't need the complete information on each sign, but make sure your phone number is on each one. You may want to put the home address on the last sign. This will bring buyers to your home where they will see the open house time, and be able to pick up a brochure. You might also consider changing "CREATIVE FINANCING" to "HOME OWNER FINANCING" or one of the other techniques you choose to use.

For Sale Brochures

Making a sales brochure is really pretty easy these days. You can create one with Microsoft PowerPoint, Excel or Word. I also have links in my website that will give you some other sources for brochures. Whichever method you choose, here are a few tips.

- Make two types of brochures; one for your yard sign and to use at your open house, and a second, a bulletin board brochure, for your local market or gas station. Make tear off tabs with your phone number at the bottom or side of the bulletin board brochure. I'm sure you've seen these in your local market.
- Look online at real estate sites to see some typical brochures and choose a layout that works for you. Any one of these headings; "Creative Financing", "Home Owner Financing", "Poor Credit Ok", "Low Down Payment", "Owner pays closing costs" will attract more buyers than other homes in your area.
- In addition to the regular statistics such as number of bedrooms, baths, or square footage; be sure to list what you consider your homes best features. Some examples of these are:

    - Basement
    - Central Air
    - Den / Office
    - Dining room
    - Family room

- Fireplace
- Forced Air
- Hardwood Floors
- Gourmet Kitchen
- Horse Facilities
- RV / Boat Parking
- Laundry Room
- Main Floor Bath
- Spa / Hot Tub
- Swimming Pool
- Exercise / Gym Area
- Security Features
- Marble Floors
- ADA Access
- Walk-in Closets
- Corner Lot
- Cull-de-Sac
- Golf Course Lot
- Waterfront
- City Lights View
- Mountain View
- River View
- Ocean View
- Gated Community
- Senior Community

All of the FSBO Sites on my website have additional information on designing and printing sales brochures as well as other items that might help you such as For Sale by Owner Signs, Open House Signs, Brochure Holders, Lock Boxes, and more. Browse through them and see what works best for you.

www.davepinvestments.com

Bulletin Boards

If you live in a Rural Area; Bulletin Boards in your local market, convenience store, gas stations, etc . . . are great places to advertise your home for sale. Here are some suggestions in using these that will draw people to your brochure.

- Notice which area of the bulletin board attracts your attention first; and put your brochure in this part of the board.

- Be sure the area around your brochure is clean of clutter.
- Use a tear off type brochure
- Check these boards regularly to see if your brochure needs replacing.
- Repeat these steps each time you check it, making sure it always draws your focus to it.

Internet Advertising

There are many internet sites that you can use to advertise your home for sale. Many of these are free, and over 80% of people looking for homes start shopping the internet first. It's through the internet that you will expand your buyers to include people relocating for work or retirement. Baby boomer retirements are approaching quickly. Take advantage of this huge group of potential buyers by making sure you have ads running outside your city. Many people move to different states when they retire. Don't ignore the people that move for work. Here are a few of the most popular internet sites you may consider placing an ad.

www.Craigslist.com

Craigslist is an excellent free source to both view homes in your area and list yours for sale. It is one of the biggest and most popular for sale sites on the internet. Look under 'housing / real estate for sale' to get an idea of what is selling in your area, and how people are wording their ads. You can also post several pictures of your home on this site.

If you want to make sure people see your ad, keep it in the first few pages of listing. Do this by checking on your ad regularly. If it is slipping down further than you want; delete it, and resubmit it. This will bring it near the top of the list once more.

www.ebay.com

Although eBay is not free, it is an excellent source for advertising your home sale. EBay charges an insertion fee when the property is listed; and a final value fee when the property is sold. They have complete instructions in their 'Sell/Seller Information Center'.

www.blogger.com

This is another free method. You can also create a blogger page with pictures of your home, a description, and your contact information. Be sure to include a Google map link on the free blogger page.

For Sale by Owner Sites

The next step up in advertising is to list your home on one of the 'for sale by owner sites'. There are many that exist to help people sell their own home. Most have a number of services to help you of which some of these are also free. I have links for some of the best and most popular ones in my site:

www.davepinvestments.com

CHAPTER 5

Professional Help

EVEN THOUGH YOU are selling your 'Home by Owner' you may still need the assistance of some professionals. I am listing the most common ones. You may want to line these up as you begin your process.

Mortgage Broker

This is the next secret. Finding a good Mortgage Broker may be the most important asset you have to selling you home quickly. They can give you the huge benefit of getting the Poor Credit or Cash Challenged Buyers approved. And since these are the buyers that will pay top dollar, and will allow you to sell your home quickly, you certainly do want the ability to work with this group. You will also get a great deal of satisfaction knowing you helped someone get the home of their dreams that might not have been able to without your help.

Nothing stops you from calling Mortgage Brokers until you find one that works with poor credit or limited cash buyers. Also find one that you feel very comfortable working with. They will be important to your success! Here are the steps you should follow: Research all the mortgage companies that advertise to Credit Problem clients. Simply Google the key words "sub-prime FHA and your City". You need a good, experienced Broker to get your buyer qualified and to be able to sell your home quickly.

You are looking for a Mortgage Broker, not a lender. Ideally, you want to find someone that works with several lenders. They will be able to find the best program for your borrower. This will typically be a government loan program, such as FHA.

Here are some of the questions you should ask when you talk with a Mortgage Broker:

- What is the lowest credit score you can get approved. You will find some can get loans approved for borrowers with credit scores in the high 500's or low 600's.
- Ask them to fax you a mini loan application. You need the paper application. You do not want your buyers going to the mortgage broker website and fill one out. This lets you keep control of the sale until you're ready to have the buyer work directly with your mortgage broker.
- Ask them what programs they have with little or no down payment. Ask if they have programs that will allow you, as the seller, to pay closing costs, or help with the down payment. They will be happy to explain what they can do.
- How much could you help with a down payment?
- What closing costs could you pay?
- Ask them if they know of any other ways you can help someone qualify.

The conversation you have with your broker will help greatly in their ability to get buyers qualified.

Title, Escrow Company, or Attorney

Depending on your State, you will use a Title Company, Escrow Company, or Attorney to close your sale. A good way to find your State requirement is to search online within your State, or look in your phone books yellow pages. Do you find Title or Escrow Companies? If neither, your State probably requires Attorneys assistance to close.

Title companies will also let you know what forms you need for closing in your State. The FSBO sites included on my site have the necessary forms for by State, as well as assistance in filling them out. I also have samples of many of the documents you need at the back of this book.

Attorney

Even if your State doesn't require an attorney; you may want one to help with the paperwork and help make the buyer feel comfortable with the transaction. It will give you both the confidence everything is done correctly. There are many attorneys available online these days at very reasonable prices.

Of course I have links in my site that I have personally used for some of my transactions.

www.davepinvestments.com

CHAPTER 6

Buyers

Knowing Your Buyers

K NOW YOUR BUYERS! Here are some nationally published statistics. Over 80% of Americans have credit problem issues and over 95% of the credit problem buyers have the funds for the normal down payment and closing costs. Out of the buyers that do have a good credit rating, only 1% will like a home well enough to buy it. This is one of the reasons it takes months, sometimes years to sell a home.

Knowing this, and knowing what to do to qualify the buyers that are in the poor credit situation, is a huge advantage you now have over others selling homes in your area. You may be the buyers chance to purchase the home of their dreams; your home!

Financial Advantage to working with Poor Credit Buyers

Let's compare buyers from a financial benefits point of view. The following table contains some normal statistics on selling homes to good credit buyers through a real estate company. You can expect to undergo these expenses.

Percentage	Activity
5% to 10%	Price reduction in negotiations with buyers
5%	Repairs before Sale
3%	Closing Costs
1%	Selling Costs
6%	Real Estate Commission
20 to 25%	*Total*

Here are some financial advantages when you are selling your own home and working with poor credit buyers

- You can sell your home at top appraised value of similar homes in your area. You have saved the 5% to 10% in negotiations
- Buyers are much more willing to accept the home and terms without having a lot of upgrades. You can add another 5% savings for the typical repairs or upgrades.
- Of course you save the 6% in real estate commission

The costs you might incur by selling your own home and working with credit challenged buyers

Percentage	Activity
Zero	Price reduction in negotiations with buyers
< 1%	Repairs before Sale
3 to 6%	Closing Costs (with you helping the buyer)
1%	Selling Costs
Zero	Real Estate Commission
0 to 3%	Down Payment Assistance
5 to 11%	*Total*

Let's discuss each of these:

- Price reduction in negotiations with buyer: It will probably not be necessary for you to adjust your asking price as you are helping the buyers qualify for the loan, and they will be grateful to pay full price for the dream of owning their own home.

- Repairs before sale: Although this could be zero, I have put in 1% as an estimate just in case you have minor repairs. These will probably be cosmetic, paint, etc . . . If you do them yourself, the cost should be minimal.
- Closing Costs: In addition to paying the required sellers closing costs, you can help with some of the buyers closing costs, up to 3%. Look at *www.fha.com* to see what costs you may assist with.
- Selling costs: the Normal 1% Seller Costs will still apply.
- Of Course with you selling by owner, there will be no Real Estate Commission.
- Down Payment Assistance. Some loan programs will allow the seller to assist with the down payment, up to 3%. Although, this is usually reserved for the buyers with good credit, but limited cash.

You can see pretty quickly the financial advantages of you selling your own home, and to credit challenged buyers are considerable. It is well worth your effort! And I haven't included the time-to-market of selling to this group of buyers. With these methods, you may be able to have your home sold in a few weeks!

Finding Buyers

Let's look at typical buyers that will be drawn to the ads I'm asking you to place. These are buyers with challenged credit that don't feel they have the credit or income or time on the job or some other requirements to qualify for a home loan. They may have cash, or not have cash, but because of the many loan programs, I will show you what you can do to find the resources to qualify these buyers to buy your home.

Managing the Buyer Process

One of the first things you want to do to manage the buyer process is to have a message on your voicemail. Explain if they are calling with interest in the home, you are having an open house. If they will leave you their name and number, you will call them back with an appointment for a showing at one of your open houses. If you have caller id, use it to call them back even if they don't leave a message.

Remember I said at the beginning of this book that it is very important you know your customer. The initial phone conversation is critical to this. You want to accomplish a couple things during this first conversation.

- See if they are someone you can work with. In other words; you're going to 'pre-qualify' them to buy your home.
- Get them to come to your open house

There are a couple important rules to remember when talking to your potential buyers.

1. The person who calls has the control of the conversation. So, if you are answering the phone, ask for a name and phone number, and call them back. This gives you the control.
2. The buyer will start out asking questions about the house. You need to take control of this conversation as well. The easiest way to do this is to simply ignore their question and start asking your own. After you get your questions answered, start answering some of theirs. But remember, you want them to come to your open house. So end the conversation as soon as you each have enough information to make an appointment. Although you will be tempted to tell them everything about the house; don't! The open house is where you will answer all their questions, and close the sale. If you give them too much information now; they will be less apt to come to the open house.

Here are some of the questions you should ask at the phone conversation.

1. Ask if the need help with financing.
    This will help you to get the rest of the conversation headed in the right direction.
2. Ask when they need to move?
    If you want to sell your home quickly; don't talk to someone that doesn't expect to move right away. You be the judge of how soon is soon enough, but you certainly don't want to wait six months for someone to sell their home first.
3. Ask where they live now, and how what their rent or mortgage payment is. The important question is really the second one. This will let you know if they can afford the payments on your home.

4. Let them know you're not too concerned about credit. What is important is the amount of down payment they are able to make. Ask how much down have they set aside? If it's enough that you can work with the loan programs you've found; let them know it sounds like something you can work with. This will boost their confidence immensely, and will certainly get them to your open house.

    Even though you may be concerned with credit later on, don't try to make decisions based on this up front. Remember, you have the ability to work with credit challenged buyers.

5. Can you afford $1,200 (or whatever you anticipate the payment would be) per month? Be sure to included taxes and insurance in your monthly payment estimate. Most loan programs require this to be impounded as part of the payment. Obviously, you want a "yes" answer to this question.

Now, let them know when your open house is. Ask them if that will work for them. If not, let them know when the next one is, and so on. Make sure they have directions to your home. Also let them know you think they have a good chance. If you don't do this, they will start thinking about the questions you've asked, and get discouraged. You want to keep their excitement at a high level.

CHAPTER 7

Holding Open House

Getting People to your Open House

O NE OF THE techniques to get people to your open house is to have the message with the open house times on your voicemail. The advantage here is that you're not trying to answer all their questions over the phone. You want them to come to your open house, and you will be very happy to answer all their questions then. Remember, they need you in order to buy a home. You will have plenty of buyers.

Setup

Have a brochure close to the front door to hand your buyer when they arrive. Have clipboards with mini-applications and pens ready for them to fill out following their walkthrough of your home. These can be kept on the kitchen counter, dining table, or coffee table. Close to where you want to sit and have a conversation with them.

Here are some little open house tricks. Replace light bulbs with 75 watt bulbs, and turn them on during the showing. Even if it's during the day! Open all curtains. Light brightens a home; darkened homes may look dingy, boring, and small. Have soft music playing, especially in the bedroom. Spray the home with room freshener, or have a couple scented candles burning. If you have a pet, make sure they're out of the house during the showing.

If you can, find some developer open houses to walk through. See if you can pick up on any 'tricks of the trade' they may be doing. Again, you need to stand out with something different from the other homes in your area.

Buyer Arrival

Greet the buyer at the door with a handshake and hand them one of your home brochures. Have something handy to write their name and something about them, so you can remember them later.

After the introduction, invite them to look around and tell them you'll be glad to help with any questions. Unless your home is empty, you should accompany the buyers on the walkthrough. Stay out of their way though, and do not try to explain everything to them. Only answer questions at this point.

After they have seen the house, invite them back to the place you have the mini-application. Now is the time for you to emphasize the qualities of the home you would like them to know about. Talk about things like extra insulation, double paned windows, hardwood floors, upgraded appliances, new roof, good schools, quiet neighborhood, etc . . .

Getting the Application Filled Out

Ask them "Do you like the House?" And, wait for an answer. Most likely, the conversations will always lead to financing. Simply ask them to have a seat, and you will explain what you're looking for and how you may be able to help them. Let them know you have special financing available, and that your main interest is finding someone with a good steady job.

Find something you like about the buyer(s), and let them know you like that. This helps them feel they have a good chance of being selected. If you have already received an offer or two, you should let them know you have other offers. This will also work in your favor. Now, have them fill out the application. Be sure to review the application for completeness before they leave.

Following your open house, fax your applications to your loan broker for pre-approval. Keep in mind getting a loan approval is a numbers game. Many of your potential buyers will not get approved; even with special programs and loans you've found. Once you do have approval, move quickly to the Sale Agreement filled out and signed, and accept some earnest money. Note: Always have the earnest money check made out to your title or escrow company. If the buyer backs out of the contract for any reason other than the loan fails, you are entitled to keep those funds. However, if the reason is loan failure you must return the money.

Do not have your buyers working directly with the loan broker until you have received the pre-approval, and a signed sale agreement, and have received earnest money. You have spent the time and effort to find a broker that can approve credit challenged customers, this is the primary advantage you have over other sellers, and you certainly don't want to lose this power.

Now, have your buyers work directly with the loan broker for the rest of the process. See Chapter 8, 'Qualifying Buyers' for the list of required documents. Explain to them, gathering this documentation ahead will help speed up the process when they start working with the Loan Officer.

CHAPTER 8

Qualifying Buyers

L OAN COMPANIES USUALLY require a 40% debt to income ratio. This is calculated on the gross income. However, there are a couple items that could possibly be dropped from this calculation. For example; if they are within six months of paying off a consumer loan such as an automobile, it can be dropped from the debt calculations. A good Loan Broker may be able to help boost a credit score 20 or 30 points immediately by knowing some of this information.

Loan Brokers

Of course, if your buyer is pre-qualified for a loan, and has cash for the down payment and closing costs, you can skip this part. In this chapter, I will show you how to qualify the credit or cash challenged buyer.

Realize at this point, through the loan programs and mortgage brokers you have found, and using the techniques in this book; you are the buyer's best chance of getting a loan approved and purchasing the home of their dreams. This is what allows you to get top dollar for your home, without having to reduce the amount as you might for pre-qualified buyers.

You should not attempt to qualify your buyers for a loan yourself. This is the job of the loan broker and in most States you need to be a licensed loan officer to do this. You can however, get a mini application from your loan broker, have the customer fill it out, and fax it to your loan broker. By doing this, you keep the loan process in your control until the buyer has been pre-qualified, at which point you have them sign the sale agreement, and give you earnest money in the form of a check made out to your Escrow or Title Company. Then, and only then, have them work directly with the loan broker. If you connect them with the loan officer before having the contract of sale and earnest money; they can use your loan broker to purchase property elsewhere.

Loan Checklist

These are the items your borrower will need to complete a government loan process. Buyers can be prepared to provide some information to your loan officer. Having your buyer get it ready now may save time later.

- Address to their place of residence (past two years)
- Copy of Drivers License and Social Security card
- Names and location of their employers (past two years)
- Gross monthly salary at their current job(s) and one month worth of paystubs
- Copies of social security, pension, and/or retirement award letters
- Pertinent information for all checking and savings accounts with three months of bank statements
- Pertinent information for all open loans
- Complete information for other real estate they own
- Approximate value of all personal property
- Certificate of Eligibility and DD-214 (for veterans only)
- Current check stubs and W-2 forms (past two years)
- Personal tax returns (past two years), current income statement and business balance sheet for self-employed individuals
- In some cases, they may need to pay for a credit report and appraisal of the property.

Some borrowers may also need the following:

- Explanation of any credit derogatory
- Bankruptcy and discharge paperwork
- Divorce decree and any settlement paperwork if applicable

CHAPTER 9

Credit Repair

THERE COULD BE some things holding your buyers credit score down that could be corrected quickly. Some of these can be implemented quickly enough they could bring the score up to qualify for your home. Others will take longer, but would certainly help them longer term.

1. Your buyer should correct any inaccuracies on the credit by cleaning up any errors in personal information such as wrong addresses, social security numbers, and employment information.
2. They should review any negative credit information and correct errors. Credit reporting agencies have 30 days to verify an item and respond to the inquiry or remove it from the report.
3. Credit card balances need to be less than 35% of the total card limit. Of course this can be accomplished by lowering the balance, but it might also be accomplished by calling the companies and having the credit limit increased.
4. They may be able to call the creditors and negotiate a lower interest rate. This will immediately lower the monthly payment and help with the overall debt to income ratio.
5. They may also be able to call their creditors and get late fees, over limit fees removed.

6. The number of inquiries brings the score down; so these should be kept to a minimum.
7. Six to twelve months of paying on time will raise the credit score.
8. If the buyer is in collections right now; they may be able to call the creditor and arrange a payoff. Some creditors will delete the collection from the report. Although, this usually depends on the types of loans. Creditors are usually not allowed to delete credit card loans, but are allowed to delete doctor and medical bills.

CHAPTER 10

Loan Programs and Qualifications

FHA

THE 203(B) FHA Fixed Rate Mortgage Loan Program is probably the most used FHA home loan, especially among first time home buyers. This loan keeps the down payment and closing costs to a minimum. The 203(b) FHA loan will finance up to ninety-seven percent of the loan. The Buyer must qualify with some debt-to-income ratios, but this loan does not have a minimum income requirement.

FHA Guidelines

FHA Loan Guideline change constantly. I will give you some of the primary ones, but be sure to check *www.fha.com* for current, and much more detailed, information.

FHA Mortgage Limits

The first thing you should do is see if your home price falls into the FHA Guidelines for Loans in your area. Check my site for a link to do this.

Simply enter your State and look through the list of Counties, or enter your specific County. For example: when I enter Michigan it returns the mortgage maximum for a single family residence of $271,050 to $345,000 depending on the county.

On the other hand, if enter Hawaii, the site returns a maximum loan amount from $618,750, to $790,000 depending on the county.

Credit Score

So you've verified the home is priced within the FHA Limits. Let's talk about the Credit Score. You may be surprised to find out there is no minimum credit score to qualify for a FHA Loan. However, there are some requirement differences based on the credit score, and Lenders have their own minimum scores to make loans. This is why it is important you find a Loan Broker that specializes in FHA Loans, and that works with several lending institutions. This will absolutely be your best chance to get a borrower approved.

FHA borrowers must have a minimum credit score of 580 to qualify for the most favorable down payment plan, which is currently at 3.5%. Borrowers with credit scores of less than this will require at least a 10% down, but may still be able to find financing.

Mortgage Insurance

In addition to the Down Payment, Buyers must also pay an upfront Mortgage Insurance Premium. This is calculated by multiplying the base loan amount by a percentage rate (which is currently at 2.25%). But, if the new FHA Reform Act passes the Senate (which it is expected to) some of the upfront payment can be shifted to the annual mortgage insurance premium. This gives the borrower more time to save, and make room for the Mortgage Insurance Payment in their budgets. Check the FHA Site to see if 'House Resolution 5072, the FHA Reform Act' has passed.

Qualifying Ratios

HUD limits a borrower's monthly mortgage payments to 29% of their gross monthly income. A borrower's total debt (proposed monthly payment plus monthly payments towards credit cards, student loans, car payments, and other installment and revolving credit) cannot exceed 41% of their gross monthly income.

Here's how these are calculated:

1) MORTGAGE PAYMENT EXPENSE TO MONTHLY INCOME

Add up the mortgage payment (principal and interest, escrow deposits for taxes, hazard insurance, mortgage insurance premium, homeowners' dues, etc.). Take the amount and divide it by the gross monthly income. The maximum ratio to qualify is 29%. *See the following example:*

Total amount and new house payment: $750
Borrower's gross monthly income (including Spouse, if married) $2,850
Divide total house payment by gross monthly income: $750/$2,850
Debt to income ratio equals 26.32%

2) TOTAL FIXED PAYMENT TO GROSS INCOME
Add up the total mortgage payment (principal and interest, escrow deposits for taxes, hazard insurance, mortgage insurance premium, homeowners' dues, etc.) and all recurring monthly revolving and installment debt (car loans, personal loans, student loans, credit cards, etc.). Then, take that amount and divide it by the gross monthly income. The maximum ratio to qualify is 41%. See the following example:

Total amount and new house payment: $750
Total amount of monthly recurring debt: $400
Total amount of monthly debt $1,150
Borrower's gross monthly income (including Spouse, if married) $2,850

Divide total monthly debt by gross monthly income: $1,150/$2,850

Debt to income ratio equals 40.35%

Borrower Documentation Requirements for FHA Loan

See Chapter 8 'Qualifying Buyers' for the list of documents required for an FHA Loan

Closing Costs

Closing costs for FHA home loans are around 2% or 3% of the total mortgage. One advantage when taking out an FHA loan is mortgage terms may allow the borrower to build in closing costs into the mortgage. While FHA requirements define which closing costs are allowable as charges to the borrower, the specific costs and amounts that are deemed reasonable and customary are determined by each local FHA office. All other costs are generally not allowed and are usually paid by the seller.

- Lender's origination fee
- Deposit verification fees
- Attorney's fees

- The appraisal fee and any inspection fees
- Lender's origination fee
- Cost of title insurance and title examination
- Document preparation (by a third party)
- Property survey
- Credit reports (actual costs)
- Transfer stamps, recording fees, and taxes
- Test and certification fees
- Home inspection fees up to $200

Down Payment Assistance

Down payment assistance programs were possible until President Bush signed H.R. 3221, The Housing and Economic Recovery Act of 2008. Part of this act banned seller-funded down payment assistance programs which allowed the seller to contribute towards the closing costs and down payment of FHA loans. For first-time homebuyers, down payment assistance programs helped make getting that first home with an FHA loan even more affordable. There is hope; a bill called the FHA Seller-Financed Down payment Reform Act of 2009, introduced in January 2009 by Representative Al Green (D-TX) and 17 co-sponsors.

The bill is designed to, "revise the requirements for seller-financed down payments (also known as SFDPA) for mortgages for single-family housing insured by the Secretary of Housing and Urban Development under title II of the National Housing Act," according to OpenCongress.org.

However, the 2009 FHA Seller-Financed Down payment Reform Act has not been passed or rejected yet. Until changes to the law are passed by the federal government, down payment assistance programs are still banned.

Other FHA Loan Programs

Depending on your situation; it may be worth your while to look at some other FHA Loan Programs.

FHA home mortgages also include FHA loans for a "fixer-upper" home. This is the FHA Loan 203(K). This loan combines the purchase price of the house and the cost of repairs. There are also FHA loans available for qualified borrowers over the age of sixty-two, to convert a portion of the equity in a home into cash.

There are FHA loans available for mobile homes and manufactured homes. In addition to the other types of FHA loan guidelines that pertain to specific types of purchases, there is also the FHA Energy Efficient Mortgage, also known as EEM, providing mortgage insurance to buy or refinance a residence and include the cost of energy-saving upgrades.

For an FHA Energy Efficient Mortgage, the borrower isn't required to qualify for the extra money needed to include the energy upgrades, and there is no down payment required for the extra amount.

Some of the other types of loans available through FHA.com are balloon loans; construction to perm loans; relocation mortgages; bridge and equity loans; specialty products for lower down payments, larger properties and self-employed income; credit solution loans for credit issues; expanded ratios; alternative income sources; and down payment options.

Other Types of Loans

VA Fixed Rate Loans

In 1944, President Franklin D. Roosevelt signed the Servicemen's Readjustment Act into law. This bill, known as the GI Bill, allows veterans to purchase homes without making a down payment. The VA Fixed Rate Loan gives borrowers the option of financing their mortgage in 15, 20, 25, or 30 year terms with the interest rate remaining fixed for the life of the loan.

A VA Loan is guaranteed by the Department of Veterans Affairs and can be used to purchase a single family home, including a townhouse or condominium unit in a VA approved project, to build a home, and purchase and improve a home. The Loan is assumable under certain conditions and does not have a prepayment penalty.

VA financing is designed to benefit veterans of the armed services, those currently in active duty or the reserves, and their spouses. In order to qualify for a VA loan veterans must be eligible as defined by the Department of Veterans Affairs. Currently, veterans can qualify to put zero down on a loan up to $417,000. Before closing, a funding fee must be collected from the borrower and can be financed into the loan. A funding fee exemption is possible upon proper verification of disability.

Conventional Fixed Rate Loan

A Conventional Conforming Fixed Rate Loan is fixed in 15, 20, 25, or 30 year terms with the interest rate remaining fixed for the life of the loan. This loan follows the strictest guidelines for eligibility in terms of loan amounts. It is not assumable and may not contain a prepayment penalty.

Jumbo Fixed Rate Loan

A Jumbo Fixed Rate Loan is different from other loans in that it is designed specifically to accommodate mortgage amounts in excess of $333,700. Due to their higher dollar amount, Jumbo loans generally carry a higher than average risk to the lender therefore interest rates may be higher. The interest rate on Jumbo Fixed Rate

Loans corresponds to a 15, 20, 25, or 30 year term and the interest rate remains fixed for the life of the loan. This loan is not assumable.

Alternative A Fixed Rate Loan

An Alternative A Fixed Rate Loan is designed to help people who are in need of customized financing because of the unusual characteristics of their loan transactions. This is a fixed rate loan that carries the option of a 15 or 30 year term and the interest rate remains fixed for the life of the loan. This Loan is not assumable and does not contain a prepayment penalty.

CHAPTER II

Creative Financing

Financial Assistance to Buyers

T HE MOST STRAIGHT forward method of creative financing is to simply be willing to pay closing costs or help with the down payment if the type of loan allows.

Second Leans

Another way you may want to help yourself and your buyer is to take back a second lien for some portion of the sale price. Lenders may make a loan of 80% to 90% based on the Loan-to-Value and allow the seller to carry a second lien note for the difference between the required down payment and their LTV.

When a buyer refinances or sells; they must pay off any second note(s). Therefore, your second lien can be turned into a full cash-out in the future.

Risks of carrying a Second Lean

Under normal situations carrying a second is pretty safe since anytime the homeowner refinances, or sells, the second must be paid in full from escrow. The danger is if the home is sold short or on a tax sale, the second lien could suffer. The sequence of payouts from escrow is taxes and tax liens, then First Mortgage, then

Second Mortgage, etc . . . However, carrying a second does give you some other flexibility. For example: If the buyer defaults on the second, you may simply tell them not to worry about it, that you'll collect (including interest and penalties) when the home is refinanced or sold.

You can find examples of seconds, and the appropriate forms on the FSBO Sites I have given you. If you do carry a second; you should have an attorney review it.

www.davepinvestments.com

Note Loans

Another possibility is to sell the loan to a Note Buyer. This is one of the things that would allow you to advertise Owner Financing. Note: The key is 'having the ability' to work with Note Brokers. It doesn't mean you must do this to advertise "Owner Financing". There are Investor Clubs or Web-Sites that advertise Note Buyers. Working with them is similar to working with a Loan Broker. Loan Applications, and other documents are very similar, and they will replace the Loan Broker in the Closing Process. Look up "Investor Clubs" or "Residential Note Buyers" online. These will of course be at much higher interest rates than conventional loans.

CHAPTER 12

Signing the Contract

CONGRATULATIONS! YOU RECEIVED the initial loan approval, and are ready to sign the Sales Contract. You should have received the details of the Contract, such as final loan amount, down payment, interest rate, and monthly payment, from the Loan Broker when you received the initial loan approval.

You'll want to complete the Sale Agreement prior to calling your buyer to set up a meeting. This will avoid having missing information at the time you meet that could require another meeting, or delay the process.

Call your buyer and schedule a meeting at your home or a central location. Some Title and Escrow Companies will let you use an office or conference room. Sign the Sales Agreement, and have them fill out an earnest money check made out to the Title or Escrow Company. At this time, you can have them contact your Loan Broker and complete the Loan Process.

Be sure to call your Broker, and let them know you have signed the Sale Agreement; that you have a check for the earnest money, and that you have told the buyer to contact them to complete the Loan Process.

CHAPTER 13

Closing Process

FINAL CLOSING IS the event where the home is paid for and title will transfer to the new buyer. The transfer is done by the seller(s) signing a deed for the buyer(s) to record the transfer of ownership. This is also the point the keys will be turned over to the new home owner!

Title Company, Escrow Company or Attorney's Office

Whether you are using a Title Company, Escrow Company, or Attorney's Office, the process for submitting the final paperwork is the same. Take the Sales Contract, Earnest Money, and any other documentation you have to your Closing Representative. The Title Company will let you know what additional requirements they have. These could include.

- Survey
- Termite or Insect Inspection
- Asbestos, Mold, or Radon Inspection

The Title Company, Escrow Company, or Attorney's Office will give you a receipt for the Earnest Money and will begin the closing process. The first step in the process will be to cash the Earnest Money Check. This will verify the Funds are available.

Let your Broker know you have started the Closing Process and where this is being done. This will let them know they can process their side of the transaction to the same company. At this point, you can sit back and relax! Hopefully, everything will go smoothly.

CHAPTER 14

Other Options

I F YOUR HOME has been on the market for some time, and you are still not able to close your home sale; there are a couple other options you may wish to consider.

Lease to Own

This is another method that will allow you to advertise owner financing. In the lease option, you are usually working with borrowers that have the down payment, but their credit does not allow them to get a loan at this time. The lease option will allow you to 'sell' them the home while they get their credit score raised. Of course their down payment, and monthly lease payment, will help in raising their score.

There are companies that will manage the lease for you for an initial setup fee and a monthly management fee, which are usually quite low. The Lessee will pay the lease payment to the management company, and they will deposit it to your account. Search the Internet for "Lease Management Companies" in your area to obtain detailed services and fees. Many can help you with a 'Lease to Buy' form as well.

If you do decide the Lease-to-Own option is for you, there are a couple additional things you might want to do.

Personal Property Lean

Establish a UCC1 Lien. This is a lien against the buyer/tenants personal property that is inside the home. Write a list of the contents of the house and file a UCC1 lien against these items. The proper way to do this can be found on the internet. Simply search on 'how to create a UCC1 Lien'.

Contact the Secretary of State's office of the debtor's residence to determine if that office accepts UCC-1 Financing Statements. Most states require the UCC-1 to be filed there. However, a few may require the UCC-1 to be filed in the county recorder's office where the debtor resides or in the county where the personal property subject of your lien may be located. Here are some steps you should follow:

1. Download the appropriate form of the UCC-1 required by the filing office where the debtor resides or personal property is located. There is an easy-to-find version of the UCC-1 identified as the "National UCC Financing" that will most likely be accepted by any filing office. However, some offices use modified UCC-1s and it is good practice to use the modified form to ensure your lien has the full benefits of filing.
2. When filling out the UCC-1, give special attention to correctly identifying the debtor's information, especially name spellings, alternate names, and identifying the personal property subject to your lien.
3. Follow the filing instructions provided by the filing office. You will probably have the option of filing the UCC-1 in person or by mail. Some offices may offer online filing.
4. Be sure to verify the length of time your UCC-1 is valid. Most state laws provide for the expiration of a UCC-1 five years from the date of filing. However, you can normally extend the period for another five years by making an additional filing before the UCC-1 expires. Your filing office will have a form for this.

Landlords Insurance

You should also have Landlords Insurance. This is to cover expenses if the lease falls through, or the renter moves out leaving property damages behind. Landlords Insurance will cover these damages or missing items, such as stoves or refrigerators.

Selling to Investors

If you are in need of a real quick sale, and you have enough equity to do this; you may want to sell to an investor. This is certainly not the best option for most people, since many investors expect a 40% to 50% discount. You can find Investors by:

- Searching the internet for Real Estate Investor Clubs or for Real Estate Investors in your area
- There may be some listed in your local newspapers

CHAPTER 15

Sample Forms

THERE ARE GENERALLY only a few forms you need to sell your home. For most States these are:

- Offer to Purchase
- Real Estate Sales Contract
- Residential Disclosure Statement
- Lead Based Paint Disclosure (if your home was built prior to 1978). You can find information on this in EPS – Lead Based Paint Information pamphlet: *http://www.hud.gov/offices/lead/enforcement/disclosure.cfm*

You may be able to find these forms for free through the internet, your library, or Title Company. But for a few dollars; the sites I've suggested in this ebook have done the research for you and have packaged the necessary documents required for your State. You can purchase by individual forms or a complete package.

www.davepinvestments.com

For Your Convenience, I am including a description and the information required in each of the forms:

Offer to Purchase Form

Although this is naturally filled out by the Buyer, it does require both theirs and your signatures.

A standard purchase offer form may be used in all states in the U.S. Any special conditions regarding the purchase should be included here as well.

Below is some of the basic information needed in a real estate purchase offer form.

- **Full names of the buyer and the seller.**
- **Address and legal description of the property.**
- **The offer price for the house.**
- **Terms of payment and the down payment amount.** This specifies how they will finance the purchase of the property if it's through a mortgage loan or other options. If the Buyer is prequalified, that should also be included.
- Include the amount and form of the earnest money deposit. This serves as a proof that they are serious in purchasing the property.
- **Expected date of transferring title and possession of the property.**
- **Responsibilities of the seller in terms of a clear title transfer and deed type.**
- **Information as to which personal properties are included in the sale.**
- **Time frame for acceptance of the offer.**
- **Provisions for a final home inspection before closing.**
- Requirements that may be specific to your state or location are also included in the form.
- Contingencies, such as who pays the closing costs, owner move out date, title transfer date, financing terms, and home inspections, are written above the signature block

Real Estate Sales Contract

A Real Estate Sales Contract must contain the following:

- **Identify the parties:** Both the Seller(s) and the Buyer(s) are required
- **Selling Property:** At least the address; preferably the legal description must be on the contract.
- **Purchase price:** The amount of the sales.
- **Include signatures:** all parties involved in the sale must sign.
- **Have a legal purpose:**

- **Involve Competent Parties:** Mentally impaired, drugged persons, etc. cannot enter into a contract. Contracts in which at least one of the parties is a minor are voidable by the minor.
- **Reflect a meeting of the minds:** Each side must be clear and agree to the contract.
- **Include Consideration:** Money is the most common form of consideration, but other consideration of value, such as other property in exchange, or a promise to pay is also satisfactory.

Real Estate Process

Real estate contracts are usually formed by one party making an offer and another party accepting the offer. The offers and acceptances (purchase agreement) must be in writing and signed by the parties agreeing to the contract.

The person making the offer prepares a purchase agreement, signs it, and transmits it to the seller. The seller may accept the offer by signing it, reject it, make a counteroffer, or choose not to respond in the requested time period. All but the acceptance will terminate the offer. This process can continue indefinitely until the seller agrees or the buyer withdraws.

To be legal, the final contract must possess original signatures by the parties and any alterations to the contract must be initialed by all the parties involved.

Contingencies

Although it is possible for a real estate contract to not have contingencies, most of them will. Some of the contingencies that are typically in a contract include:

- Mortgage contingency – Purchase of the real estate is contingent on or subject to the buyer getting financed.
- Inspection contingency–Purchase is contingent on passing inspection with no significant defects.
- Another sale contingency – placed on the sale of purchase of other real estate.
- Appraisal contingency – Purchase is dependent on the amount a lender will loan on the home

Condition of property

A real estate contract usually states the condition of the home at the time of the new owners' possession. It may say sold as is, or it may represent a warranty for the condition of the house, fixtures, and appliances. This is where a 'disclosure form' is sometimes used. It may also include what personal properties will stay with the home, such as sold with washer and dryer.

Riders

Riders are special attachments that become part of the contract

Earnest money deposit

Earnest money usually accompanies the purchase offer. The amount is listed in the contract with the remaining balance of the sale amount to be paid at closing.

Residential Property Disclosure Statement

I have included a typical Disclosure Statement. This may be a little different depending on your State. In most States, the seller must complete, sign and date this disclosure form and deliver it to the buyer as soon as practicable, but no later than before an offer is accepted by the Seller. If the seller becomes aware of a defect after delivery of this statement, but before an offer to purchase is accepted, an amended disclosure statement should be prepared with the newly discovered defect to the purchaser.

The declarations and information contained in this disclosure statement are not warranties, express or implied of any kind, and are not a substitute for any inspections or warranties the purchaser may wish to obtain. The information contained in this disclosure statement is not intended to be a part of any contract between the purchaser and seller. The information and statements contained in this disclosure statement are declarations and representations of the seller and are not the representations of the real estate licensee.

Instructions to the Seller: (1) Answer ALL questions. (2) Report known conditions affecting the property. (3) Complete this form yourself. (4) If some items do not apply to your property, circle N/A (not applicable). If you do not know the facts, circle Unk (unknown). (5) The date of completion by you may not be more than 180 days prior to the date this form is received by a purchaser.

LOCATION OF SUBJECT PROPERTY: _____
SELLER IS __ IS NOT __ OCCUPYING THE SUBJECT PROPERTY.
Appliances/Systems/Services: (The items below are in **NORMAL** working order)
Circle below Circle below

Sprinkler System	N/A	Yes	No	Unk
Swimming Pool	N/A	Yes	No	Unk
Hot Tub/Spa	N/A	Yes	No	Unk
Water Heater	N/A	Yes	No	Unk
___Electric ___Gas				
___Solar				
Water Purifier	N/A	Yes	No	Unk
Water Softener	N/A	Yes	No	Unk
___Leased ___Owned				
Sump Pump	N/A	Yes	No	Unk
Plumbing	N/A	Yes	No	Unk

	N/A	Yes	No	Unk
Whirlpool Tub	N/A	Yes	No	Unk
Sewer System	N/A	Yes	No	Unk
___Public ___Septic				
___Lagoon				
Air Conditioning System	N/A	Yes	No	Unk
___Electric ___Gas				
___Heat Pump				
Window Air Conditioner(s)	N/A	Yes	No	Unk
Attic Fan	N/A	Yes	No	Unk
Fireplaces	N/A	Yes	No	Unk
Heating System	N/A	Yes	No	Unk
___Electric ___Gas				
___Heat Pump				
Buyer's Initials Buyer's Initials				
(OREC-11/03)				
Humidifier	N/A	Yes	No	Unk
Gas Supply	N/A	Yes	No	Unk
___Public ___Propane				
___Butane				
Propane Tank	N/A	Yes	No	Unk
___Leased ___Owned				
Ceiling Fans	N/A	Yes	No	Unk
Electric Air Purifier	N/A	Yes	No	Unk
Garage Door Opener/Control	N/A	Yes	No	Unk
Intercom	N/A	Yes	No	Unk
Central Vacuum	N/A	Yes	No	Unk
Security System	N/A	Yes	No	Unk
___Rent ___Own				
___Monitored				
Smoke Detectors	N/A	Yes	No	Unk
Dishwasher	N/A	Yes	No	Unk
Electrical Wiring	N/A	Yes	No	Unk
Garbage Disposal	N/A	Yes	No	Unk
Gas Grill	N/A	Yes	No	Unk
Vent Hood	N/A	Yes	No	Unk
Microwave Oven	N/A	Yes	No	Unk
Built-in Oven/Range	N/A	Yes	No	Unk
Kitchen Stove	N/A	Yes	No	Unk
Trash Compactor	N/A	Yes	No	Unk

Seller's Initials Seller's Initials

LOCATION OF SUBJECT PROPERTY

Source of Household Water
___Public ___Private ___Well Yes No Unk
Other Items_____ Yes No Unk
Other_____ Yes No Unk
Other_____ Yes No Unk

IF YOU HAVE ANSWERED NO to any of the above, please explain. Attach additional pages with your signature(s).

_____

_____

Zoning, Flood and Water Circle below

1. Property is zoned: *(Check one)* ___residential ___ commercial
    ___historical ___ agricultural ___ industrial ___ office
    ___urban Conservation ___ other ___unknown
2. Are you aware of any flood insurance requirements concerning the property? Yes No Unk
3. Do you have flood insurance on the property? Yes No Unk
4. Has the property been damaged or affected by flood, storm run-off, sewer backup, drainage or grading problems? Yes No Unk
5. Are you aware of any surface or ground water drainage systems which assist in draining the property, e.g. french drains? Yes No Unk
6. Has there been any occurrence of water in the heating and air conditioning duct system? Yes No Unk
7. Are you aware of water seepage, leakage or other drainage problems in any of the improvements on the property? Yes No Unk

Additions/Alterations/Repairs

8. Have any additions or alterations been made without required permits? Yes No Unk
9. Are you aware of previous foundation repairs? Yes No Unk
10. Are you aware of any alterations or repairs having been made to correct defects or problems? Yes No Unk
11. Are you aware of any defect or condition affecting the interior or exterior walls, ceilings, slab/foundation, basement/storm cellar, floors, windows, doors, fences or garage? Yes No Unk
12. Has the roof ever been repaired or replaced during your ownership of the property? Yes No Unk

13. Approximate age of roof, if known _____Number of layers, if known_____ Unk
14. Do you know of any current problems with the roof? Yes No Unk
15. Are you aware of treatment for termite or wood-destroying organism infestation? Yes No Unk
16. Do you have a termite bait system installed on the property? Yes No Unk
17. If yes, is it monitored by a licensed exterminating company? *(Check one)* ___ yes ___ no Annual cost $ _____
18. Are you aware of any damage caused by termites or wood-destroying organisms? Yes No Unk
19. Are you aware of major fire, tornado, or wind damage? Yes No Unk

Environmental

20. Are you aware of the presence of asbestos? Yes No Unk
21. Are you aware of the presence of radon gas? Yes No Unk
22. Have you tested for radon gas? Yes No Unk
23. Are you aware of the presence of lead-based paint? Yes No Unk
24. Have you tested for lead-based paint? Yes No Unk
25. Are you aware of any underground storage tanks on the property? Yes No Unk
26. Are you aware of the presence of a landfill on the property? Yes No Unk
27. Are you aware of existence of hazardous or regulated materials and other conditions having an environmental impact? Yes No Unk
28. Are you aware of existence of prior manufacturing of methamphetamine? Yes No Unk
29. Have you had the property inspected for mold? Yes No Unk
30. Have you had any remedial treatment for mold on the property? Yes No Unk
31. Are you aware of any condition on the property that would impair the health or safety of the occupants? Yes No Unk

Property Shared in Common, Easements, Homeowner's Association, Legal

32. Are you aware of features of the property shared in common with adjoining landowners, such as fences, driveways, and roads whose use or responsibility has an effect on the property? Yes No Unk
33. Other than utility easements serving the property, are you aware of easements or right-of-ways affecting the property? Yes No Unk
Buyer's Initials _____ Seller's Initials _____

LOCATION OF SUBJECT PROPERTY

34. Are you aware of encroachments affecting the property? Yes No Unk

35. Are you aware of a mandatory homeowner's association? Yes No Unk
    Amount of dues $ _____ Special Assessment $ _____
    Payable: *(Check one)* ___monthly ___ quarterly ___annually
    Are there unpaid dues or assessments for the Property? *(Check one)* ___ yes ___no
    If yes, amount $_____Manager's Name:_____
    Phone No._____

36. Are you aware of any zoning, building code or setback requirement violations? Yes No Unk

37. Are you aware of any notices from any government or government-sponsored agencies or any other entities affecting the property? Yes No Unk

38. Are you aware of any threatened or existing litigation or lawsuit(s), directly or indirectly, affecting the property? Yes No Unk

39. Is the property located in a fire district which requires payment? Yes No Unk
Amount of fees $ _____ To Whom Paid _____
    Payable *(Check one)* ___monthly ___quarterly ___annually 40. Is the property located in a private utility district? Yes No Unk *(Check applicable)* water ___garbage ___sewer ___ other ____ If other, explain: _____
    _____ Initial membership fee $ _____ annual membership fee $ _____ If more than one (1) utility, attach additional pages.

Miscellaneous

41. Are you aware of other defect(s), affecting the property, not disclosed above? Yes No Unk

42. Are you aware of any other fees or dues required on the property that you have not disclosed? Yes No Unk

If you answered "YES" to any of the items 1-42 above, list the item number(s) and explain. *(If needed, attach additional pages, with your signature(s), date(s) and location of subject property.*

On the date this form is signed, the seller states that based on seller's **CURRENT ACTUAL KNOWLEDGE** of the property, the information contained above is true and accurate.

Are there any additional pages attached to this disclosure *(circle one):* **Yes No. If yes, how many?**_____

Seller's Signature Date Seller's Signature Date

> **A real estate licensee has no duty to the Seller or the Purchaser to conduct an independent inspection of the property and has no duty to independently verify the accuracy or completeness of any statement made by the seller in this disclosure statement.**

The Purchaser is urged to carefully inspect the property and, if desired, to have the property inspected by a licensed expert. For specific uses and restrictions for this property, contact the City Planning Department. The Purchaser acknowledges that the Purchaser has read and received a signed copy of this statement. This completed acknowledgement should accompany an offer to purchase on the property identified.

Purchaser's Signature_____ Date _____

Lead Based Paint Disclosure

Lead Warning Statement

Every purchaser of any interest in residential real property on which a residential dwelling was built prior to 1978 is notified that such property may present exposure to lead from lead-based paint that may place young children at risk of developing lead poisoning. Lead poisoning in young children may produce permanent neurological damage, including learning disabilities, reduced intelligence quotient, behavioral problems, and impaired memory. Lead poisoning also poses a particular risk to pregnant women. The seller of any interest in residential real property is required to provide the buyer with any information on lead-based paint hazards from risk assessments or inspection sin the seller's possession and notify the buyer of any known lead-based paint hazards. A risk assessment or inspection for possible lead-based paint hazards is recommended prior to purchase.

Seller's Disclosure

(a) Presence of lead-based paint and/or lead-based paint hazards (check (i) or (ii) below):

   (i) _____ Known lead-based paint and/or lead-based paint hazards are present in the housing
   (explain).

   _____

   _____

   (ii) _____ Seller has no knowledge of lead-based paint and/or lead-based paint hazards in the housing.

(b) Records and reports available to the seller (check (i) or (ii) below):

   (i) _____ Seller has provided the purchaser with all available records and reports pertaining to lead based paint and/or lead-based paint hazards in the housing (list documents below).

   _____

   _____

   (ii) _____ Seller has no reports or records pertaining to lead-based paint and/or lead-based paint hazards in the housing.

Purchaser's Acknowledgment (initial)

(c) _____ Purchaser has received copies of all information listed above.

(d) _____ Purchaser has received the pamphlet *Protect Your Family from Lead in Your Home.*

(e) Purchaser has (check (i) or (ii) below):

    (i) _____ received a 10-day opportunity (or mutually agreed upon period) to conduct a risk assessment or inspection for the presence of lead-based paint and/or lead-based paint hazards; or

    (ii) _____ waived the opportunity to conduct a risk assessment or inspection for the presence of lead-based paint and/or lead-based paint hazards.

Agent's Acknowledgment (initial)

(f) _____ Agent has informed the seller of the seller's obligations under 42 U.S.C. 4852d and is aware of his/her responsibility to ensure compliance.

Certification of Accuracy

The following parties have reviewed the information above and certify, to the best of their knowledge, that the information they have provided is true and accurate.

_____

Seller Signature   Date

_____

Purchaser Signature   Date

www.ingramcontent.com/pod-product-compliance
Lightning Source LLC
Chambersburg PA
CBHW021908170526
45157CB00005B/2015